TRIAL

IN

THE

WOODS

T0152208

Trial in the Woods
© 2021 Stephanie Barber

Published by Plays Inverse Press
Pittsburgh, PA
www.playsinverse.com

ISBN 13: 978-0-9997247-8-1

Cover Art by Jackie Milad
Design by Tyler Crumrine
Printed in the U.S.A.

**PLAYS
INVERSE**

TRIAL IN THE WOODS

A PLAY IN TWO ACTS BY
STEPHANIE BARBER

PLAYS INVERSE PRESS
PITTSBURGH, PA
2021

CAST OF CHARACTERS

BEAR CHONDRA. Exercise instructor

JUDGE BODON BOAR. The judge

PROSECUTOR LYNX. Prosecuting attorney

DEFENSE SQUIRREL S. Defense attorney

OVELIA OTTER. Defendant in the case

PENNSTIN THE YOUNG WOLF. Victim of the crime

REPORTER ELLE E. PHANT. Television reporter

OFFSTAGE CAMERA PERSON. Elle E. Phant's camera person, always a voice offstage/off-camera

TURTLE. Member of the jury, had attended class, some sort of stoned

BISON. Member of the jury, had attended class, some sort of stoned

LIZARD. Member of the jury, had attended class

TIGER SEPET. Member of the jury, had attended class, uptight

HARRISON HARE. Member of the jury, had attended class, uptight

FERN CARDINAL. Member of the jury, had attended class

ELMOND FOX. Eyewitness from class

MS. HARWOOD OWL. Eyewitness from class, very sexual

ELIJAH WOLF. Character witness, sister of the victim

LOUIS MACAQUE. Expert witness on screams, cries, whines, vocalizations, etc.

ZINNIA SNAKE. Eyewitness from class

BUCK DIVINE. Eyewitness from class

MR. SHELLSCAPE. A character witness

SCENE

A clearing in the forest.

TIME

Present day.

ACT I | SCENE I

SETTING: *We are in a clearing in the woods.*

AT RISE: *The whole class of animals is focused in a deep squat, lifting alternate legs and arms, swinging—steady, repetitive focused exercise in unison.*

BEAR CHONDRA

(speaks with a low, calm, authoritative, and kind voice, encouraging while also transcendent) Okay, you all look beautiful. Scales and fur and paws and hooves AR-TIC-U-LAAAAA-TED. Yes, every element of your body is separate and united. Feel that? Connected and alone. Just like you, circling the sun alone. Circling the sun with each other and with every twig and tree and ocean and stone. Stay with it. Use your core and stretch and stretch and stretch and stretch and kick and kick. You're getting your heart rate up but you are also slowing your mind. Slow those gamma waves. And always stretching and expanding and growing and loosening. You are teaching yourself that you can stay with it. Stay with hard times. Stay with it even when you are tired. Stay with it when you are bored. Stay with it when you wish only to dash off into a strawberry patch and roll in the sunshine of gods' eternal love. Stay with it as you get stronger and calmer and cooler. Feel the pain burning up your sex, rock a little, yeah, rock.

BEAR continues in exercise-monologue voice while doing a slow, sexy grind, not campy.

Burn. Get lower. Get down on the floor. Get down in the soil where you'll be soon enough. Feel that pain as a reminder of your coming death. A reminder of your current state of aliveness. Ummmmm. Alive, yeah…

BEAR and class go up on toes.

Lift your head up, place the tippy-top of your head exactly over your neck, your neck exactly over your spine. Tuck your tail in just a bit and stretch yourself up to the heavens and puuuulll yourself down to the earth. In ballet all the dancers' motions are away from the earth, they are on pointe shoes so that very little of their body is touching the earth, they are reminded again and again to imagine a string pulling them from the crown of their head, pulling them towards the heavens where the European god is. In many African dances the motions are directed towards the earth, the legs are bent, the foot is flat and broad—spread and pressed against the earth, the knees are bent and the body is pressing into this earth where the African gods are, the food and the ancestors in the earth. Pull yourself down and pull yourself up. There's no right place to put your gods, animals. You'll be in the soil soon enough. You'll be in the clouds, on the wind, in your fellow's mouth and fur soon enough. Feel the pain as a reminder of your coming death.

Animals are still up on toes, with knees bent wide and arms out (goddess pose). They are focused and pained with the strain of holding the position.

Your present life. Deeper, slower. Puff your stomach

full of air and tighten your bum. Feel it? Feel it like light flowing from the ground into your sex and all the muscles that keep your sex on your body. Keep your sex on your body as you contemplate your body dissolving. Good. Tighten…endure…embrace…Your ass is going to be so high, people are going to fuck you with their ideas—right through their third eye into your gloriously strong and decaying sex.

OVELIA OTTER turns to PENNSTIN THE YOUNG WOLF and attacks her brutally, sensationally. Strobe lights flash, speed metal plays—stylized, sexualized…all other animals circle the attack and watch hypnotized, neither enjoying nor disliking, stopping nor encouraging PENNSTIN's murder. This goes on for a few minutes, with OVELIA OTTER ripping the blood and body and fur which fly everywhere as she crouches over PENNSTIN's body. All characters freeze, OVELIA over PENNSTIN, all other animals surrounding OVELIA OTTER and the body.

ALL (BUT OVELIA)
(spoken and sung) WHAT HAS HAPPENED?

HARRISON HARE
It took a minute to realize that something sensational is not always the answer to existential ennui.

TURTLE
I feel bad I got a little excited.

BISON

I feel worse I got a little wet.

LIZARD

I was scared but I did nothing to stop it.

FERN CARDINAL

(singing fully now) I was composing a poem with the effluence of sorrow emitting from both of these animals who I have known my whole life.

BEAR CHONDRA

Animals whose paws I have envied and animals whose hooves I have held.

TIGER SEPET

Animals who brought me books when I was lonely.

ELMOND FOX

Animals from whom I ran in the night.

BISON & TURTLE

Animals I enjoyed tormenting.

ALL

(spoken or sung by all animals and/or broken into duets & trios)
Animals whose detritus I lived upon.
Animals whose days I watched from air.
Animals whose feces I rolled in…rolling and rolling through the matter of both body and earth, the matter which erupts from darkest innards and summons forth the essence of an animal.

Capital A. Animal.
Who sings what is flexible.

BLACK OUT / END OF ACT.

ACT 2 | SCENE I

SETTING: *Another clearing in the woods, adjacent to what will serve as the courtroom.*

AT RISE: *REPORTER ELLE E. PHANT is speaking directly to a television news camera while FERN CARDINAL stands dazed beside her, TIGER SEPET stands stiffly, and ZINNIA SNAKE wanders behind them with disinterest.*

OFFSTAGE CAMERA PERSON
This broadcast brought to you by a future directory.

REPORTER ELLE E. PHANT
I'm broadcasting from the scene of a horrible slaughter which occurred earlier today at Bear Chondra's Mix Flow Get Up And Go weekly exercise class in the hollow by the wishing well behind the beaver club. Yes, back there amongst the trees, a young wolf was brutally attacked and killed by an angry otter. The attack came as a surprise to the animals who regularly attend Bear Chondra's Mix Flow Get Up And Go class which has a wonderful reputation for peace and generally good-feeling feelings post, and during, class. We have a few of the attendees here.

The animals are still covered in blood.

Fern Cardinal, I understand you were standing right next to Pennstin, the young wolf that was murdered, throughout the class.

FERN CARDINAL

Yes, I spent the class next to her. She always worked hard and inspired me to stay focused and not fall into worry that I won't finish strong. She was an inspiration to us all and we will be hard-pressed to go on with the same *joie de vivre* in class next week.

REPORTER ELLE E. PHANT

Thank you, Fern.

FERN CARDINAL

(continues talking) Things happen. That's the only surety. Things happen and we were there while this was happening. Pressure is an eventuality and it is true we are all filled with blood.

REPORTER ELLE E. PHANT

Thank you, Fern. I'm going to speak to some of your classmates.

Turns to ZINNIA SNAKE.

Zinnia, I understand you are a regular participant of Bear Chondra's Mix Flow Get Up And Go class and were in the back when this incident occurred.

ZINNIA SNAKE

Mmmmmm. Mmhhhh. Yeah. That was some shit. I sort of feel like Fern though. I mean, is everything gonna be understood? We're animals…this whole arresting and reporting, I mean, I don't know what we're playing at. Regulating and blaming and making up gods and making up rules and reasons. We're not scared like the humans. We know it's all wack and we're not trying to convince ourselves it ain't.

REPORTER ELLE E. PHANT

Thank you, Zinnia, and lastly let's hear from Sepet. Sepet, were you able to witness the incident?

TIGER SEPET

Yes, but I'm uninterested in speaking about this with you.

REPORTER ELLE E. PHANT

Okay, thank you. We'll be covering the trial and will bring you the most up-to-date news as it breaks.

BLACK OUT / END OF SCENE.

ACT 2 | SCENE 2

SETTING: *Another clearing in the woods set up to mimic a courthouse.*

AT RISE: *PROSECUTOR LYNX standing to address JUDGE BODON BOAR who sits center stage while BISON, LIZARD, TURTLE, TIGER SEPET, HARRISON HARE, and FERN CARDINAL sit to the side and listen as jury.*

PROSECUTOR LYNX

Your honor, esteemed members of the jury, I am saddened and, indeed, outraged to be requesting your assistance in assuring justice prevails amongst our sacred circle here in the forest. I intend to present evidence which proves, beyond a shadow of a doubt, that on the 5th gibbous moon Ovelia Otter, in front of many witnesses, brutally and without cause attacked and killed the young wolf Pennstin at Bear Chondra's Mix Flow Get Up And Go exercise class at the wishing well. You, the reasonable jurors and members of our well-balanced forest community, will be convinced of the malice and utter cruelty of the attack. Furthermore, I believe you will be convinced of the need to remove Ovelia from our society. I'm sure you will agree that there is no space for senseless murder in our community, no space for the psychological morbidity and illness so regularly attributed to the human species—the tide of which we have, in great part, been able to stem here in the wily but wise woods. The *mens rea* will be established and an aggravated assault guaranteed recognizable. You, serious and concerned members of the jury, will have no choice but to convict and protect the balance of the forest from such aberrant behavior.

DEFENSE SQUIRREL S.

Good afternoon, your honor, and thank you, jurors, for your selfless service to the health of our complicated populace. As my worthy colleague, Prosecutor Lynx, has outlined and, as you, of course, were already aware, a sorrowful death has befallen our commonwealth. We will all mourn the loss of young wolf Pennstin and our hearts and sympathies and deliberate assistances go out to Pennstin's family and dear friends. But to convict Ovelia Otter of this regretful occurrence would be egregious and would, I will prove, upset the delicate, nuanced ANIMAL balance of our forest. I will prove the impossibility of such a prosecution amongst an ecosystem more complex and interdependent than something so lacking in valenced complexity as a "law"

Spoken with mocking derision.

so cruelly dismissive of the vicissitudes of brain chemicals, hormones, the weather, fast eyes, the presence of claws and teeth, the muscle memory and speed which press upon all animals who move through our lives tossed wildly between hunt and danger, hunger and satiety. Words which suggest something so rigid, so without lability as "law" have no place in animal interaction. I will prove, beyond a shadow of a doubt, that not only should this case be dismissed and the basis upon which

17

it has been erected,

TURTLE and BISON giggle.

be washed away like so many beaver dams come spring, but that, were we to abide by the restrictive codes which no animal ought, this occurrence can still not be deemed murder as *mens rea* cannot and will not be established. Ovelia Otter, who sits here amongst us now can no more be prosecuted for her alleged act than a seed be convicted, a rainstorm imprisoned, or a nautilus shell fined for spiraling out from itself in beauty and elegant mathematics. Thank you.

BLACK OUT / END OF SCENE.

ACT 2 | SCENE 3

SETTING: *A clearing in the woods outside the courthouse.*

AT RISE: *REPORTER ELLE E. PHANT is in front of the television news camera holding the microphone by her side.*

REPORTER ELLE E. PHANT

(talking to OFFSTAGE CAMERA PERSON before 'rolling') "…from the play box to the press box HBCU sports radio"…I was at the *Tallahassee Telegraph* and she was at the *Ocala Observer*…

OFFSTAGE CAMERA PERSON

We're rolling.

REPORTER ELLE E. PHANT

(in on-camera voice) Okay, okay, so we are back and we are out in front of the courthouse where we've been keeping you abreast of the happenings at the trial today. *Voir dire* has been conducted and opening remarks delivered. This sensational trial in the woods has caught fire in the forest and today we will be hearing from the Judge and, we assume, some eyewitnesses. It should make for a fascinating day.

OFFSTAGE CAMERA PERSON

We're out.

REPORTER ELLE E. PHANT

(continues in off-camera voice) And yeah, you could just tell she was going to be a star, I mean, listen to her, she's just...great...

BLACK OUT / END OF SCENE.

ACT 2 | SCENE 4

SETTING: *In the courthouse clearing.*

AT RISE: *JUDGE BODON BOAR is speaking to jury.*

JUDGE BODON BOAR

Well, jurors, the court would like to thank you for performing your civic duty. I will ask you to listen to all sides and all witnesses and refrain from forming any opinions until all material has been presented. Are you willing to agree to this stipulation?

JURORS

We are.

JUDGE BODON BOAR

Thank you. Prosecutor Lynx, please call your first witness.

PROSECUTOR LYNX

Thank you, Your Honor. I would like to call Elmond Fox to the witness stand.

JUDGE BODON BOAR

Mr. Fox, will you share your vision of the events in as truthful a manner as you are able?

ELMOND FOX

I will.

JUDGE BODON BOAR
Please proceed.

PROSECUTOR LYNX
Thank you, Your Honor, and thank you, Mr. Fox. I imagine it has been a hard time for you.

ELMOND FOX
It is true I do not appreciate violence.

PROSECUTOR LYNX
Can you confirm for the judge and jury that you were in attendance at Bear Chondra's Mix Flow Get Up And Go exercise class at the wishing well on the 5th gibbous moon?

ELMOND FOX
Regretfully, yes, I was in attendance. I appreciate Bear Chondra's cadence and encouragement.

PROSECUTOR LYNX
And where were you standing when Ovelia Otter senselessly attacked the young wolf Pennstin?

DEFENSE SQUIRREL S.
Objection!

JUDGE BODON BOAR
Certainly. Prosecutor Lynx, please contain the descriptive elements of your questioning.

PROSECUTOR LYNX
Please forgive me.

ELMOND FOX

Is it not only through such descriptions that what occurred can truly be felt by others?

JUDGE BODON BOAR

Those sorts of words are prejudicial in a courtroom, which, however childishly, hopes to establish truth through actions and facts alone.

PROSECUTOR LYNX

Of course, Your Honor.

ELMOND FOX

Well, it is not a matter of course to me. Look at me. I am fur and paws and teeth and tail. I'm no sailor setting out a course and denying the emotionalism of what I have witnessed and how I felt. Senseless is a perfect adjective. Senseless is what the prosecutor said and senseless is what Ovelia Otter did. I know so because the act was entirely without sense. Or perhaps it was all sense and no reason. All smells and sounds and sights. All heartbeats thumping and sweat forming and surprise and fear masking the true sorrow of such an event.

DEFENSE SQUIRREL S.

Objection!

ELMOND FOX

I object! I object to violence for the sake of violence. I object to the inability to conceive of new methods of conflict resolution. I object to the selfishness bred into the generations, seeping through the greed and cruelty of the human species' invention of the evil economic system of capitalism! I object to capitalism's oppression of the natural world! I object to the natural world's surrender to this abuse of power! I object to this trial

JUDGE BODON BOAR yells over these next few objections.

and the unrecognized humor of the phrase *mitigating circumstances!* I object to the patriarchal suggestions of the word *circumstances!*

JUDGE BODON BOAR
(interrupting and yelling over ELMOND FOX)
Prosecutor Lynx, please silence your witness or I will ask that he be removed from the trial!

ELMOND FOX
Feel free to remove me! Daisies and the scent of trees after a storm and sunsets and wolf pups! These have been removed from young Pennstin, why should not I be removed from the banality of this charade!

JUDGE BODON BOAR
Please step out of the courtroom, Elmond Fox, and do not return for the remainder of the trial, however much we may seem to die of boredom without your delightful antics.

ELMOND FOX
With pleasure or a distinct lack of pleasure!

DEFENSE SQUIRREL S.
I would request that Elmond Fox's rant be stricken from

the record.

JUDGE BODON BOAR

Certainly. Jury, please disregard the testimony of this first witness. Prosecutor Lynx, I hope your other witnesses will act with a bit more decorum.

PROSECUTOR LYNX

Yes, Your Honor, I am very sorry about that. I am sorry to have wasted the jury's time as well.

JUDGE BODON BOAR

Yes, yes, fine. Call your next witness.

PROSECUTOR LYNX

Thank you, Your Honor. I would like to call as my next witness Ms. Harwood Owl, who was also present on the day of the brutal and ultimately fatal attack of the kind and generous young wolf Pennstin.

DEFENSE SQUIRREL S.

I object.

JUDGE BODON BOAR

Prosecutor Lynx, once again, kindly limit your adjectives.

PROSECUTOR LYNX

Yes, Your Honor. Ms. Harwood Owl, were you present during the attack of which we are speaking today?

MS. HARWOOD OWL

(looking at JUDGE BODON BOAR sweetly) Yes, Your

Honor. I was present. I like to stay fit.

PROSECUTOR LYNX
And were you able to see the attack, Ms. Owl?

MS. HARWOOD OWL
We all watched. I watched and we all watched. I remember my mother used to touch my face so lightly when I was a young owl. When first flying, the fear was intermingled with the most pleasurable delight. Soaring and fearing and trusting and doubting all wrapped into one frenzy of motion. I miss my mother. Her scent was as the light and lifting current.

PROSECUTOR LYNX
But during class at Well Wishing Studios on the morning of the 5th gibbous moon, did you watch as Ovelia Otter brutally attacked Pennstin the young wolf?

DEFENSE SQUIRREL S.
Objection.

JUDGE BODON BOAR
Agreed, the jury will disregard the novelistic flourishes Prosecutor Lynx seems constitutionally impelled to include. Please continue.

PROSECUTOR LYNX
Owl, were you present on the day the attack was made on Pennstin the young wolf?

MS. HARWOOD OWL
Certainly, I go every week to Bear's class.

PROSECUTOR LYNX

And did you see Ovelia attack Pennstin in class that day?

MS. HARWOOD OWL

I did.

PROSECUTOR LYNX

And can you describe to us where you were standing when the attack occurred?

MS. HARWOOD OWL

Otter was in the row in front of me, a little to my left. We were squatting and pulsing for a mighty long time, Your Honor, and I was imagining a love based on radical acceptance and a quick and rounded laugh. Otter turned. We were all in it. We were all working in our bodies and our minds and thinking about Bear's words and thinking about corporeality. I think perhaps Bear and perhaps Ovelia too felt the burden of having a body as something profound and clawed. We creatures that fly are relieved sometimes of this weight.

DEFENSE SQUIRREL S.

Objection, witness is speaking to the defendant's state of mind.

MS. HARWOOD OWL

Yes, that is right. I think Otter's state of mind caused the attack. I think her state of mind murdered Pennstin the young wolf. It is hard to know just who is responsible for Ovelia Otter's state of mind. That is what we should prosecute. Otter's state of mind.

DEFENSE SQUIRREL S.
I object!

JUDGE BODON BOAR
(to prosecutor) If you are unable to produce reasonable testimony from your lovely witness I will move to have her words stricken from the transcript and ask that she be, regretfully, removed from the stand.

PROSECUTOR LYNX
Yes, Your Honor.

To MS. HARWOOD OWL.

Ms. Owl, can we proceed with solely yes and no answers for a while?

MS. HARWOOD OWL
Yes.

PROSECUTOR LYNX
Did you see Ovelia Otter attack Pennstin the young wolf during your Mix Flow Get Up And Go Fit and Focus class at the wishing well in the morning on the 5th gibbous moon of the year?

MS. HARWOOD OWL
Yes.

PROSECUTOR LYNX
And were you standing to the right of the altercation?

MS. HARWOOD OWL

Yes.

PROSECUTOR LYNX

And how long would you say this altercation lasted?

MS. HARWOOD OWL

(silent)

PROSECUTOR LYNX

Oh, yes, forgive me. Witnesses from your class that day have stated that the altercation lasted approximately 5 minutes. Would you agree with that time?

MS. HARWOOD OWL

Yes.

PROSECUTOR LYNX

Did you witness Pennstin the young wolf in any way provoking or threatening Ovelia Otter before the beginning of this attack?

MS. HARWOOD OWL

No.

PROSECUTOR LYNX

Have you got any knowledge as to why Ovelia Otter might be compelled to attack Pennstin?

MS. HARWOOD OWL

No.

PROSECUTOR LYNX
So it is your belief that, unprovoked and unthreatened, Ovelia Otter violently took the life of Pennstin for absolutely no reason?

DEFENSE SQUIRREL S.
Objection!

JUDGE BODON BOAR
Jury, please strike the statement.

PROSECUTOR LYNX
So, Owl, you were aware of no reason why Otter would attack Pennstin during class?

MS. HARWOOD OWL
Yes. Or, no.

To JUDGE BODON BOAR.

Can I say one small thing here?

JUDGE BODON BOAR
Yes.

MS. HARWOOD OWL
Yes, I am NOT aware of a reason. Or NO I am not aware of a reason. I don't know how to say it properly. I am not aware and I was not aware. I do not know why any of that happened but I really do not know why anything happens. It is a thought I find comforting. I do not know and I cannot know.

JUDGE BODON BOAR
(looking lovingly at MS. HARWOOD OWL) Yes. It is difficult to comprehend our existence.

MS. HARWOOD OWL
(returning look of love to JUDGE BODON BOAR) Yes.

PROSECUTOR LYNX
No more questions, Your Honor.

JUDGE BODON BOAR
Squirrel S., your witness.

DEFENSE SQUIRREL S.
Do you feel absolutely certain you witnessed this attack?

MS. HARWOOD OWL
Yes.

DEFENSE SQUIRREL S.
Even though, as an owl, with a fascinating but distinctly different way of seeing and hearing the world...I, a squirrel, cannot be sure that what I consider certainty... certain vision, certain sound, certain motion and time and spatial surety, are the same visions, sounds, and awarenesses that you would rely on as truth. These certainties, when viewed from different eyes and different perspectives, may look entirely different.

PROSECUTOR LYNX
Objection, Your Honor. The defense is presenting arguments. Specious and intellectually clumsy, but arguments nonetheless.

DEFENSE SQUIRREL S.

Withdrawn. Owl, can you be certain that what you took as true, what you saw that day at the wishing well was in fact the truth of the occurrence as every animal would recognize it?

MS. HARWOOD OWL

No, I suppose I cannot.

DEFENSE SQUIRREL S.

No more questions, Your Honor.

JUDGE BODON BOAR

(lovingly) Thank you, Ms. Owl, your assistance in the trial has been greatly appreciated.

MS. HARWOOD OWL

(with equal love) Thank you, Your Honor, I enjoyed the process immensely.

JUDGE BODON BOAR

Let's take a 5-minute recess. Ms. Owl, can you speak with me in my chambers?

TIGER SEPET

This is highly unprofessional.

LIZARD

I find it positively electrifying, the way the shadow of doubt which Defense Squirrel S. inserted into the proceedings got the judge and Owl all turned on. This thing is really picking up.

BISON

Yeah, that was hot.

TURTLE

(chewing) Word.

TIGER SEPET

Unbelievable!

BLACK OUT / END OF SCENE.

ACT 2 | SCENE 5

SETTING: *A clearing in the woods outside the courthouse.*

AT RISE: *REPORTER ELLE E. PHANT is in front of the television news camera holding the microphone by her side.*

REPORTER ELLE E. PHANT

(speaking before rolling) …well, I never would have gone for a small if he weren't standing there beside me.

OFFSTAGE CAMERA PERSON

3, 2, 1, rolling…

REPORTER ELLE E. PHANT

It's been an exciting morning at the courthouse. The testimony of Elmond Fox and Ms. Harwood Owl has cast some doubt on what had previously been considered the one known fact about this trial. We felt certain the Otter HAD at least attacked and killed young Pennstin the wolf. What hadn't been known was *why* and if that *why* could be enough of a reason to excuse her actions. Okay, the judge is returning. I'll keep you posted here on FPT, Forest Public Television.

BLACK OUT / END OF SCENE.

ACT 2 | SCENE 6

SETTING: *In the courthouse clearing.*

AT RISE: *JUDGE BODON BOAR reenters the courtroom, all rise. Judge sits, all sit.*

PROSECUTOR LYNX
Your Honor, instead of my next eyewitness I would like to present Pennstin's sister, Elijah, to remind the jury and the courtroom what we have lost in the death of Pennstin.

JUDGE BODON BOAR
Will you be returning to your eyewitness list afterwards?

PROSECUTOR LYNX
Yes, sir.

JUDGE BODON BOAR
Defense?

DEFENSE SQUIRREL S.
I have no objections to this attempt to muddy the waters with saccharine emotionalism in an effort to lay blame on one individual when we all know the motors of our existences are elsewhere.

JUDGE BODON BOAR
Very well, proceed.

PROSECUTOR LYNX

Your Honor, I call to the stand Elijah Wolf of the deep western patch near the 7th ridge.

ELIJAH WOLF steps to witness box.

Elijah, can we expect your adherence to the truth as you understand it?

ELIJAH WOLF

You can.

PROSECUTOR LYNX

Elijah, I would like to begin by expressing my deepest condolences for you and your family's loss.

DEFENSE SQUIRREL S.

Objection.

PROSECUTOR LYNX

Very well. Ms. Elijah, I understand that you sometimes attend Bear Chondra's exercise class.

ELIJAH WOLF

Mm hhhhhmmm, that's right.

PROSECUTOR LYNX

And why did you decide not to attend last week?

ELIJAH WOLF

I don't know. You know? I woke up and I was just, I was tired. I was a deep sort of tired, don't have nothing to do with working or partying the day before. I was some sort of caustic tired and, to tell the truth, I been tired ever since that morning.

To JUDGE BODON BOAR.

I don't suppose you superstitious, judge, or what ain't superstitious but may be just being deep open to other clues and signs. I been like this since always, not Pennstin. She just, you know. She blithe. She was blithe. But that's why people liked her so much. She was the type of wolf everyone like. That's not me. I'm, oh, I'm not meaner or nicer than she was, I'm just not as easy and quick with everyone. I'm too…

She makes shaky electrical moves with her paws.

ZZZZZZZZZ. I think people like you better when you're less aware of them. They like it better you ain't looking too hard cuz your eyes set on yourself.

DEFENSE SQUIRREL S.
Objection. Relevance?

ELIJAH WOLF
Electricity very relevant, Your Honor.

JUDGE BODON BOAR
Can the prosecution establish relevance?

PROSECUTOR LYNX
I'm hoping Ms. Elijah can give us some insight into Pennstin's life and impact on the community and environment.

JUDGE BODON BOAR

A more direct line of sight would be preferable.

PROSECUTOR LYNX

I understand. May I proceed?

JUDGE BODON BOAR

Proceed.

PROSECUTOR LYNX

So, Elijah, you are testifying that Pennstin was the sort of wolf who was liked by many. Can you speak to her impact on the environment?

ELIJAH WOLF

Oh yes, sir. I mean, forever. Pennstin was on the right path. A narrow path which don't trample too many weeds, don't disturb the soundscape, don't disregard the lace-like nature the forest got. Woods is interwoven, you know. Me and Pennstin apex, sure, but that don't mean we don't know we part of the whole. Wolves run tight. We family and organized and we communicate. That's how we get things done and that's how we so deep in the concept of holism. Lot of us work together to get a big bison.

BISON

(from the jury box, like he just put together that it wasn't a coincidence) Oh, huh! Ok.

ELIJAH WOLF

Or caribou, something big. What mostly goes down is we just wind up with the weakest or the oldest of these biggies cuz that's who slow down or get left behind. Then we pretty fair and save some for a mom didn't come out hunting with us or some cubs. What it is is we eat everything we kill. We don't just kill and right there, that's it. That's all you got to understand about wolves. I eat every bit I can or I share it with my pack. The bones I leave behind feed the lammergeier and the bones she don't eat fertilize the soil. The rich limestone, calcium hydroxyapatite helping all the seedlings get tough and big. Then those seedlings grow big trees and some tasty little fox curl up in the hole at the trunk of one of those trees and you see? You see how it's a circle? It's that what Bear Chondra's always talking about. It's just common decency to take just what you gonna use. Not take just for the thrill or take and hoard away.

DEFENSE SQUIRREL S.
Objection. I do not believe this judge and jury require a lesson in common decency.

PROSECUTOR LYNX
I would argue this whole case is about common decency.

JUDGE BODON BOAR
I'll allow it. Prosecutor Lynx, please continue.

PROSECUTOR LYNX
So Elijah, have you ever witnessed Pennstin killing an animal that she did not intend to eat or share with her pack? For "sport," as it were?

ELIJAH WOLF
Oh no, sir. No wolf do that. Unless maybe they insane

and no wolf insane.

DEFENSE SQUIRREL S.
Objection. That statement is clearly a logical fallacy.

PROSECUTOR LYNX
The witness is not arguing the case but simply stating her beliefs. She will leave that arguing to me.

JUDGE BODON BOAR
I'll allow it. Prosecutor Lynx, please continue.

PROSECUTOR LYNX
Elijah, you've painted a very clear picture of Pennstin's importance in and respect for the environment in which she lived. Can you speak a bit about her impact on her personal community?

ELIJAH WOLF
Like on the pack?

PROSECUTOR LYNX
Yes, your pack and perhaps the other animals your pack affects.

ELIJAH WOLF
I think I done that. But, yeah, she was a great hunter. She was young so she ain't had no pups yet so I don't know about her mothering but I bet she'd be good. She was fast and she was fair and she always brought meat back to the nursing moms and the elders ain't go out to the hunt. She was strong and we tussled some over the choicest meats but that's how wolves eat. She never

ate more calories than she need and she never waste no meat or hurt nothing she don't mean to eat. She was a good one for making jokes too. We sisters but we not from the same litter and she a some moon's cycs younger than me. I don't know for sure. But close. So when she was real young and first being brought out hunting she came with me and my littermates and, you know, we were new too and not so great at it really. We were circling this big old moose. He was a guy was around the forest forever. Good sort of moose but slowing down. We was all circling the moose but we were a little disorganized and so me and Zawa and Aye and Reese was all on one side of the moose and Pennstin was small and alone on the other side. And you know that ain't how it should be. We was all to blame. But Pennstin, I don't know if she was giving up and making jokes or making jokes just cuz she was a fun one but she started clowning like her paws all been snapped by snapping turtles. She would pick one up and then the other and she was making some sounds with each play snap. What'd'ya know it worked! That moose so confused by Pennstin's little dance he turned towards her and slowed down and we three on the other side laid in and got the kill. That moose was big and a lot of meat but a little chewy cuz time done made the muscle tight. Pennstin was so cute. She brought home such a big chunk of meat for mom and the new litter and showed 'em all her snapping turtle dance and all the real little pups done start hunting with the snap-snap dance. Also Pennstin moved pretty. We all felt glad to see the pretty way she moved with all that speed and accuracy. Even when clowning she moved pretty.

PROSECUTOR LYNX

Thank you, Elijah. No further questions, Your Honor.

JUDGE BODON BOAR

Defense?

DEFENSE SQUIRREL S.

Thank you, Your Honor. Yes. Elijah, thank you for talking to us about Pennstin. This has been very enlightening to me and I'm sure has been helpful to the jury in establishing a clearer sense of just who and how your sister was.

ELIJAH WOLF

I'm happy to help.

DEFENSE SQUIRREL S.

I'm impressed by your tales of Pennstin's young guile and skill at the hunt. And your clear depiction of the pack's way.

ELIJAH WOLF

Thank you.

DEFENSE SQUIRREL S.

I wonder, Elijah, if you feel that four young wolves hunting an old and feeble moose is "fair."

ELIJAH WOLF

I don't know it's fair. What's fair? We hunting something to feed our family. Moose do the same. Grazing and eating grasses all day. Whatever else they eat. Fair ain't the forest. I mean, that's not how we do it. We do what's right and necessary. Fair something different…

DEFENSE SQUIRREL S.

But, you say it is "right" to trick a gentle, old moose, a longtime member of the forest community, because you feel that feeding your family is more important than that creature's life?

ELIJAH WOLF

Wolves hunt, that's our business. I don't know your business…you all the judiciary. I ain't got Pennstin no more whether Otter guilty or not guilty. Whatcha gonna do? Put her in a otter jail? Probably there some bacteria in her brain or something messed up at the river where she lives or with her family or with the forest outta whack. I don't know. I'm mad at her. I might try'n eat her, I can't say, but I don't know, this game you playing going to put an end to critters going freak out and hurt each other no reason. Or maybe there's a good reason we can't see. We all just seeing what we can see and that is not too much. Don't make me do your work for you. I'm just here talking about my sister. I remember her paws so smart and I used to love them pressed up against my back when we sleep. I think Pennstin was a dreamer cuz her paws just working all through the night.

Moves paws like a kneading cat.

BLACK OUT / END OF SCENE.

ACT 2 | SCENE 7

SETTING: *A clearing in the woods outside the courthouse.*

AT RISE: *REPORTER ELLE E. PHANT is in front of the television news camera holding the microphone by her side.*

REPORTER ELLE E. PHANT
(off-camera) Well, that was the way daybreak did her in, I don't think I could have been much help.

OFFSTAGE CAMERA PERSON
Rolling.

REPORTER ELLE E. PHANT
So, we are outside the courthouse after some stirring testimony from Pennstin's sister, Elijah. Elijah was brought in by the prosecution to soften the judge and jury's hearts to the loss of Pennstin but it seems she has strengthened the case for the defense. I'd like to speak for a moment to Buck Divine, who has been watching the trial and who was also in Bear Chondra's Mix Flow Get Up And Go exercise class on the day of the attack. Buck, how do you feel Elijah's testimony affected the trial's proceedings?

BUCK DIVINE
Yes, hello, Ms. Phant, thank you. Ummm, yes. I felt it was a grave misstep on the part of Prosecutor Lynx. Elijah is a well-known, deeply learned, and radical social

theorist and most anyone who follows the "Forest First" blog knows of her radical views. My guess is someone in the prosecutor's office is going to get canned today.

REPORTER ELLE E. PHANT
Yes, I suppose it seems as though it was an avoidable error. We'll just have to see if Lynx can bounce back from this significant blow. And are you expecting to be called to the witness stand?

BUCK DIVINE
Yes, I've been told I am on the eyewitness list but, I've also been told that things in a trial change. I'm very nervous as I've never been to a trial before, let alone spoken at one. I really hope I am believable and I hope I don't have too many lines to memorize and I hope the lights are not too harsh in my eyes. Which are very sensitive.

REPORTER ELLE E. PHANT
Okay, well, Buck, thank you for speaking with us. I'm sure you'll do fine. We'll continue our coverage tomorrow as the trial continues. Thanks for watching Forest Public Television. FPT, for perspective truth!

BLACK OUT / END OF SCENE.

ACT 2 | SCENE 8

SETTING: *In the courthouse clearing.*

AT RISE: *JUDGE BODON BOAR reenters the courtroom, all rise. Judge sits, all sit.*

JUDGE BODON BOAR
Please sit. Prosecutor Lynx, are you ready to begin?

PROSECUTOR LYNX
Yes. Your Honor, I would like to call Louis Macaque to the stand as an expert witness on vocalization. Louis Macaque was also in Bear Chondra's Mix Flow Get Up And Go exercise class that day and so will be an invaluable asset in helping the jury get a clear sense of just what occurred on that horrible 5th gibbous moon.

TURTLE
(to BISON) We were all there!

BISON
(to TURTLE) Man…

PROSECUTOR LYNX
Louis Macaque, are you dedicated to the relayance of the truth which you witnessed?

LOUIS MACAQUE
I am.

PROSECUTOR LYNX

Thank you. So, to let the judge and jury recognize your special comprehension of this event, I would like you to explain your expertise and how you came to this expertise.

LOUIS MACAQUE

Certainly. I am a doctor of animal screams and vocalizations and I studied for 17 years at the Vocalization Hollow Institute with the world-famous academic Clarice Reese.

PROSECUTOR LYNX

Thank you, Louis. So, on the 5th gibbous moon you were at Bear Chondra's Mix Flow Get Up And Go weekly exercise class. Is this correct?

LOUIS MACAQUE

I was.

PROSECUTOR LYNX

And where were you standing when the attack on the young wolf Pennstin occurred?

LOUIS MACAQUE

I was in the third row during class and Ovelia and Pennstin were in the front row. But then, when Ovelia Otter pounced on Pennstin, we all, I mean everyone in the class, sort of circled around. We didn't stop it but we didn't cheer them on. It happened fast but it seemed like it happened slow. Like it took a long time and was in slow motion. I wish I had done something to stop it. Done something for both of them. And for all of us but it was like I was hypnotized.

Jurors look down guiltily.

PROSECUTOR LYNX
I do not think anyone blames you.

LOUIS MACAQUE
I blame myself and I always will. And furthermore I believe I should.

PROSECUTOR LYNX
Okay, very well, can you tell the jury about the vocalizations of young Pennstin the wolf?

LOUIS MACAQUE
During class Pennstin was panting and now and then making playful little yips and barks just like she always did. Then Ovelia jumped on her—at first she didn't make any sounds. I don't know why she didn't fight. I think Pennstin could have protected herself and I don't know why she didn't try. I think maybe she was just stunned and didn't believe it was a real attack? I mean, Bear Chondra's Mix Flow Get Up And Go exercise class has always been a safe space.

LIZARD
(from jury box) "Safe space!??" What do you think we are…humans? We are animals! We are down with the deeply radical randomness of existence. HUMANS lost their claws and muscles and senses of smell and they replace all that with laws but they're worse than us. Meaner. Baser.

JUDGE BODON BOAR

Jurors, please refrain from making comments and please do not make me ask you again. You have pledged to refrain from forming opinions until you have been given all the facts of the case. Prosecutor Lynx, please continue.

PROSECUTOR LYNX

Thank you, Your Honor. Louis, please continue.

LOUIS MACAQUE

Well, umm, yes, I was saying I don't know why Pennstin didn't fight. I was staring at her and I know she was strong and I know she was smart so why didn't she rise up and fight Otter?

PROSECUTOR LYNX

And can you speak to the sounds she made?

LOUIS MACAQUE

Yes, so, during class panting, happy yips, and barks. When Ovelia jumped on her at first she was silent (that's why I think she was stunned) and then when it became clear that Ovelia was really taking all the life and blood out of her she sent up a very lonely howl. We were in the forest all together on a sunny morning but the howl felt like the deepest, snowiest arctic tone. I could feel the moon and the snow and the deep need in her utterance, the howl calls for family and the howl calls through all generations of family. When a wolf lifts her head and sends her howl into the night the sound can travel for miles and it can travel back in time for more than seven generations. A lonely plaintive cry to her great-great-great-grandparents' parents and perhaps they heard and perhaps they are with her now?

PROSECUTOR LYNX

Your Honor, I would like to present this small bit of sound to the courtroom as Exhibit A.

A looping track of wolves howling—distant and desolate—plays from a speaker.

DEFENSE SQUIRREL S.

I object.

JUDGE BODON BOAR

I find it imperative that we engage our senses when deliberating. I'd like to hear it.

All listen.

LOUIS MACAQUE

(talks while the wolf howls play) Lupine vocalizations are quite different depending on the size of the animal, the geography of the pack, the subspecies, and the reason for the howl. Young Pennstin's howl was low and steady, long slow moans that dipped down at the end, floated above the imagined snow and then dropped gently into silence. The shape of the tone was full and promising, and as Ovelia's attack continued it grew weaker and more melancholy. "Why are you doing this to me? Where will I go now? And who will greet me, nose to nose? Breath to warm breath and understanding?"

More deep listening from all in the courthouse. Moved and focused.

DEFENSE SQUIRREL S.
Objection!! Objection!!

JUDGE BODON BOAR
To what are you objecting?

DEFENSE SQUIRREL S.
I am objecting to this Svengali-like hypnotism and demand that this recording be ceased immediately.

JUDGE BODON BOAR
Yes, I suppose you are right. Prosecutor Lynx...

PROSECUTOR LYNX
(stops recording) Yes, Your Honor. No further questions.

JUDGE BODON BOAR
Defense Squirrel S., do you have any questions for Louis Macaque?

DEFENSE SQUIRREL S.
I do, Your Honor.

JUDGE BODON BOAR
Proceed.

DEFENSE SQUIRREL S.
Louis Macaque, you mentioned that you felt sure that young Pennstin the wolf would be more than qualified to defend herself against the smaller, weaker Ovelia Otter.

PROSECUTOR LYNX

Objection, Louis Macaque has been brought to this courtroom as an expert in animal vocalization, not a fight expert.

DEFENSE SQUIRREL S.

Prosecutor Lynx, it was you who allowed this path into evidence. It is now in play and I intend to pursue this line of inquiry. Your Honor?

JUDGE BODON BOAR

Yes, this is correct, proceed.

DEFENSE SQUIRREL S.

So, is it true that Pennstin could have defeated Ovelia Otter and protected herself had she wanted to?

LOUIS MACAQUE

I do not know for sure if she would have been successful and I do not know what other beings "want."

DEFENSE SQUIRREL S.

You said yourself you felt sure.

LOUIS MACAQUE

Yes, I was curious why she did not protect herself.

DEFENSE SQUIRREL S.

Is it possible that, though we do not know the reason for the attack, perhaps young Pennstin did! Perhaps young Pennstin felt the true justice in Ovelia's attack and surrendered to her fate because it was the right path!! Perhaps Pennstin was fully aware of the crime which she committed and for which she was being rightly punished!!??

PROSECUTOR LYNX
Objection!

JUDGE BODON BOAR
On what grounds?

PROSECUTOR LYNX
On the grounds that this is ridiculous nonsense, a pure fabrication which Defense Squirrel S. is introducing to confuse the jury and which is pure confabulation set upon no truth whatsoever.

DEFENSE SQUIRREL S.
Your Honor, it is my job to explore the inference which Louis Macaque has introduced to this courtroom. He was quite right in trying to pursue the question of just WHY did Pennstin so serenely surrender to Ovelia Otter. It is a perfectly reasonable line of doubt which Prosecutor Lynx's witness has suggested, this possibility that Pennstin had done a grievous wrong and was just in her surrendering.

JUDGE BODON BOAR
I'll allow it. Please continue, Defense Squirrel S.

DEFENSE SQUIRREL S.
Thank you, Your Honor. Though I have no further questions, I am thankful that this very salient point has been brought to the awareness of the jury and I hope that they will contemplate the wrong which young

Pennstin laid on Ovelia for which she so gracefully assumed responsibility.

PROSECUTOR LYNX

Objection!!

JUDGE BODON BOAR

Yes, really, that is just going too far, Defense Squirrel S.

DEFENSE SQUIRREL S.

Withdrawn, no further questions.

JUDGE BODON BOAR

We'll take a 5-minute recess.

BLACK OUT / END OF SCENE.

ACT 2 | SCENE 9

SETTING: *A clearing in the woods outside the courthouse.*

AT RISE: *REPORTER ELLE E. PHANT is in front of the television news camera doing a strange, stretching dance.*

OFFSTAGE CAMERA PERSON
Rolling.

REPORTER ELLE E. PHANT
Well, yes, there you have it, folks. This trial keeps becoming more and more complex…just when you think it is going one way, it goes the other.

Turns her back to the camera and then turns her head back to camera.

When things are topsy-turvey…

Turns head away and then back over her other shoulder to the camera.

And you don't know where to turn…

Jumps back towards camera and does a Bob Fossey kind of sexy/awkward/aggressive dance.

TUNE IN
TUNE IN

TUNE IN
FPT
FPT
FPT

OFFSTAGE CAMERA PERSON
We're out.

BLACK OUT / END OF SCENE.

ACT 2 | SCENE 10

SETTING: *In the courthouse clearing.*

AT RISE: *All are seated around the courtroom as PROSECUTOR LYNX addresses JUDGE BODON BOAR and jury.*

PROSECUTOR LYNX
I would like to call, as my next eyewitness, Zinnia Snake.

JUDGE BODON BOAR
Very good.

PROSECUTOR LYNX
Zinnia Snake, can we expect your adherence to the truth as you understand it?

ZINNIA SNAKE
Maybe not.

JUDGE BODON BOAR
Prosecutor Lynx…

PROSECUTOR LYNX
Yes, Your Honor, please forgive me. Zinnia Snake, it is well known in the forest that snakes have a distaste for the stultifying rigidities of the concept of truth.

ZINNIA SNAKE
Yessssssssssssss…

PROSECUTOR LYNX

Will you instead simply answer some questions and the judge and jury and defense team can come to their own conclusions about truth?

ZINNIA SNAKE

Yessssssssssssss…

PROSECUTOR LYNX

So, Zinnia, you were at Bear Chondra's Mix Flow Get Up And Go class when Ovelia Otter attacked and killed young Pennstin the wolf

ZINNIA SNAKE

Yessssssssssssss…

PROSECUTOR LYNX

And could you see or had you any prior information about just why Ovelia Otter would do something like this?

ZINNIA SNAKE

No one knows what a otter is doing. They look like they playing and loving on rocks but I've hear stories. Oh did I. I am knowing a lot of things that the others might misssssing. It's cuz my persssspective is different. I got a different view, baby. I'm for peaceful and I would say that a otter ain't. I don't mind how cute they looking or how many calendars and snow globes they feature in. Hoopla is something musical but treachery is treacherous. That's what my grandmother used to say. Also she say "shit is mercury" and I don't need explain that to you all. Not here, no.

PROSECUTOR LYNX

Do you believe that what Otter did that day to Pennstin should go unpunished?

ZINNIA SNAKE

Now you are getting up on top of it. I mean, now you are getting into the matter. You are getting down with the downy underside of the problem. We've been dancing and I like the tune but the rhythms's all wrong, ain't it? I know you know it, Lynx. You know it too Squirrel S. You all gonna jury this show and make the award ceremonies you know it…ain't I, Turtle?

TURTLE

(sleepy, dazed) What?

ZINNIA SNAKE

Yesssssssssssss. What is the right, Turtle baby? They all is the right. I myself is going to go unpunished. I done decided what the way to go would be because of the space and time this light going to deliver. Not anybody wrapped in the soft leaves of the forest or the rich dark scent of the loam and all the meaning it deliver. You might want to actuate but I'm not going to sign a thing. Long time ago I done felt the tug of want, the want of something that aliveness trick us to. That want…in my case…was love. In another case might be it's revolution or owning a something or strength. Your bag gonna be what you hold, but mine, for just a minute, was love. I know I don't need to tell you what love can do to a snake soul, soul of a snake deep and winding. What the good and what the bad. And ain't that a shape we gonna construct and reconstruct? Gimme that feeling running from one part of my long body to the absolute other end. From tongue to tail I want it. From tail to tongue I want it. We in another bracket right now. You know what I mean? We in the real life bracket. Sun and soil. Water and night time. Mmmm, the night, I'm so cold.

DEFENSE SQUIRREL S.
(weary) Objection.

JUDGE BODON BOAR
Really, Prosecutor Lynx, where is this snake going?

ZINNIA SNAKE
Oh, Your Honor. I'm going right out of your here courtroom you can be sure.

Spoken as ZINNIA is leaving.

You best be thankful I'm not going right up your asshole, rearrange your macaroni…

JUDGE BODON BOAR
Prosecutor Lynx, I will not have my courtroom made a mockery of.

PROSECUTOR LYNX
Yes, Your Honor, I understand, thank you. With that in mind I would like to strike my next witness, Buck Divine, from the witness list and bring up my last witness, Bear Chondra.

JUDGE BODON BOAR
Do you have any objections, Defense Squirrel S.?

DEFENSE SQUIRREL S.

I do not.

BUCK DIVINE

(from the back of the courthouse) I've got a problem with this! I object!

JUDGE BODON BOAR

Please sit down.

BUCK DIVINE

Your Honor, I saw the whole thing! I've been waiting to testify! I know all my lines and I've been so lonely and, yes, I looked forward to being heard.

JUDGE BODON BOAR

Prosecutor Lynx, remove this distraction.

BUCK DIVINE

I am not a distraction…it is because of just this sort of sentiment that the Ovelia Otters of the world go off.

JUDGE BODON BOAR

That sounds dangerously close to a threat, Mr. Divine!

BUCK DIVINE

That is a guarantee. If we keep dismissing each other we're all at risk.

JUDGE BODON BOAR

Court will recess while Prosecutor Lynx gets his roster in order.

BLACK OUT / END OF SCENE.

ACT 2 | SCENE 11

SETTING: *A clearing in the woods outside the courthouse.*

AT RISE: *REPORTER ELLE E. PHANT is in front of the television news camera holding the microphone to her mouth.*

OFFSTAGE CAMERA PERSON

3, 2, 1, rolling…

REPORTER ELLE E. PHANT

Hello, we're here at the courthouse continuing to cover the sensational murder trial of Ovelia Otter who, it has been alleged, attacked and killed the young wolf Pennstin at an exercise class by the wishing well. And well, yes, the trial and, let's face it, the woods in general, are getting a little nervy after this long day of interrogation, examination, and rumination, and we are, it is safe to say, anxious for the final step of deliberation. It is also safe to say the forest is losing patience much like Judge Bodon Boar. We've all got work to take care of outside of this nonsense.

Touching her ear.

Okay, sounds like the judge is heading back in.

BLACK OUT / END OF SCENE.

ACT 2 | SCENE 12

SETTING: *In the courthouse clearing.*

AT RISE: *JUDGE BODON BOAR is standing to address PROSECUTOR LYNX and the courtroom.*

JUDGE BODON BOAR

Prosecutor Lynx, several of your witnesses have made a mockery of this trial and of my courthouse. I've decided to have you move to your closing arguments. I don't believe that Bear Chondra can offer any further information about what happened on that day at her studio. Defense Squirrel S., are you ready to proceed to closing arguments?

DEFENSE SQUIRREL S.

Your Honor, if I may, I would like to present a witness. I also think it is imperative that we call Ovelia Otter herself to the stand.

JUDGE BODON BOAR

Oh, yes, of course. Prosecutor Lynx, do you have any objections?

PROSECUTOR LYNX

No, Your Honor. Thank you.

DEFENSE SQUIRREL S.

Your Honor, esteemed jury, I would like to call to the stand Mr. Shellscape, a deer whose sense and sweet nature you have all known your long years in the forest.

LIZARD

There is a distinct and important difference between sweet and kind. Sweetness is nice but kindness is the real mark of a good soul.

JUDGE BODON BOAR

The jury has not been asked to weigh in yet on these proceedings. Please keep your thoughts to yourself and wait to discuss these points during deliberation.

LIZARD

Yes, Your Honor. But it is a good point, isn't it?

DEFENSE SQUIRREL S.

I find it, yes, an excellent point. Mr. Shellscape is not only sweet, which is pleasurable, if superficial, but deeply kind as well, which marks a wisdom and maturity which may perhaps resurrect the dignity of these proceedings.

MR. SHELLSCAPE moving towards the witness stand.

BISON

(to TURTLE) Did he say erect?

TURTLE

He said urrect.

They giggle.

JUDGE BODON BOAR
Mr. Shellscape, do you pledge an allegiance to the truth?

MR. SHELLSCAPE
I do, Your Honor.

JUDGE BODON BOAR
Proceed.

DEFENSE SQUIRREL S.
Mr. Shellscape, I wonder if you can tell the judge and jury the story you told me a few days ago about your birthday party some years ago.

MR. SHELLSCAPE
Yes. My mother had thrown a party for my birthday. It was a sunny day and we all met by the river. Just my mom and dad and siblings and a few animals my age. I remember smelling mint. Wild mint. A scent that must have blown in from deeper in the forest because I couldn't find any to chew on. I remember thinking how mint is like the spring. And it was a spring party. Because my birthday is spring every year. Do you all know the song about spring birthdays that goes:

Born in the spring
And the spring is already rebirth
Birth
Birth-ed
Birthed
Buds and blossoms and
Baby birds
Begin begin begin

aaaaaaaand
Are all compelled to sing…

PROSECUTOR LYNX
Objection…relevance?

JUDGE BODON BOAR
(irritably) Yes, Defense Squirrel S., where is this going and how soon will it get there?

DEFENSE SQUIRREL S.
Yes, Your Honor, I beg the court's indulgence for just another minute.

JUDGE BODON BOAR
Very well.

DEFENSE SQUIRREL S.
Okay, Mr. Shellscape, please tell us what you saw at your riverside party that spring.

MR. SHELLSCAPE
Yes, I'm sorry. I got distracted thinking of the soft wind.

DEFENSE SQUIRREL S.
It is understandable, softness is compelling.

MR. SHELLSCAPE
Well, I was given some gifts, a few berries and a daisy chain for around my neck and I was opening these up and happened to look into the river and saw the most extraordinary thing.

Long pause.

DEFENSE SQUIRREL S.
Yes, what was that thing?

MR. SHELLSCAPE
I saw Ovelia Otter and her sister asleep on their backs. Floating in the river asleep on their backs and they were holding paws. When I think about it it makes me want to cry, it was so tender. So tender as to be almost the definition of tender. When I demand of myself more tenderness in my familial and community interactions I picture these two soft paws clasped gently together on a soft spring day floating down the river.

DEFENSE SQUIRREL S.
No further questions.

JUDGE BODON BOAR
Prosecutor Lynx?

PROSECUTOR LYNX
Thank you, Your Honor, Mr. Shellscape, am I to understand that the sole purpose of your testimony here today is to tell us of a time you saw Ms. Ovelia Otter asleep?

MR. SHELLSCAPE
(flustered) Well, umm…

PROSECUTOR LYNX
Mr. Shellscape, this has been a fantastic waste of time.

Turning away.

MR. SHELLSCAPE

Prosecutor Lynx, Your Honor…I'd like to say that that memory was more than just seeing Ovelia asleep. That memory was the accumulation of the impact—the impact on me and on others—friends and family I told—an impact of visioning tenderness. Experiencing a deep and protective gentleness incarnate and the impact of that experience…of me seeing that on my days in the woods. We all do it, Your Honor. We put things out there…we put visions and feelings and ideas into each other…some don't stick around very long or make much of an impact at all and some reverberate. That floating trusting love I witnessed on my birthday was like a baptism or conversion or reading an important book. It impressed me and I brought its learning with me into the future. I know that what Ovelia Otter did at Bear Chondra's Mix Flow Get Up And Go exercise class that day made an impression too. I know a lot of that fear and confusion and anger will pass through the woods for generations but I also know she put out some good too, and I guess I just wanted it to be balanced out a bit. Or everyone to know about the good she put in the world too.

PROSECUTOR LYNX

And would you have the woods look the other way when its inhabitants are murdered for no reason? Do you believe, like Defense Squirrel S. and others in this sorry excuse for a courtroom, that it is so tediously humanesque to recognize that we can have a hand in sculpting our communities? To realize that we can exert a collective will to create a more peaceful and equitable existence for ourselves? Are you stating, for the record, that the very attempt to organize or stabilize is too referential to another species and we should therefore ignore all impulses to come to some sort of collective understanding of how we would like to construct our society? I am not talking about rights! We have no rights. Rights are an abstract concept. We have no right to safety or peace but we have a chance to try to create safety and peace through discourse and agreement. We can come to a decision as a community about how we would like our lives in the woods to be and we can outline what will and will not be accepted in the pursuit of this peace.

MR. SHELLSCAPE

Yes, I agree. I of course agree. I don't condone what Ovelia Otter has done and I am not rallying for chaos and anarchy. What I am rallying against is punishment! We are going backwards. We cannot help young Pennstin the wolf by punishing Ovelia. We cannot help her family or her community. We can also not help future Pennstins. Future victims. Punishment is no deterrent to violence. Punishment is violence. Punishment is vengeance. The vengeance of a society unable to intellectually grapple with the factors that create violence. Vengeance is for humans too busy and distracted to dig deeper and address the root causes of violence. Not just the obvious factors of poverty and systemic oppression but the most ineffable wounds of existential angst and fear. Vengeance is for the humans who make money from punishment and…

JUDGE BODON BOAR

Once again, the humans are not on trial here.

MR. SHELLSCAPE

Yes. The fear of punishment may work when a critter is young. A cub may respond to a paw across the snout or a sharp caw from a mother eagle. But the depth of illness and violence we're talking about won't be cured by punishment.

PROSECUTOR LYNX

So are you suggesting that we here, today, attempt to restructure our entire legal system? Throw out all the laws and legislation and start again?

MR. SHELLSCAPE

I am.

PROSECUTOR LYNX

And then we, what, we tell the rest of the world what the new order will be?

MR. SHELLSCAPE

We do.

PROSECUTOR LYNX

Your Honor, this is a ridiculous stunt and terrific evasion. We all see that the system has flaws. We've worked for thousands of years to attempt to address these flaws and Defense Squirrel S. is creating a terrific diversion with this sidestep. We in these woods can no more restructure the entire legal and societal order than we can change the weather. This is preposterous!

DEFENSE SQUIRREL S.

What's preposterous is our understanding that I am entirely correct: that punishment will not bring back Pennstin and neither will it deter other such abuses in the future BUT that nevertheless punish her we will because that is the way it's always been done. Effective or not.

JUDGE BODON BOAR

This whole trial was a bit more amusing when Elmond Fox and Ms. Harwood Owl were speaking.

PROSECUTOR LYNX

We are not prosecuting the prosecutorial system. We are prosecuting Ovelia Otter and as such we have offered this judge and jury clear evidence of her crime. Were we to prosecute the legal system of the forest I would have conducted my business differently.

DEFENSE SQUIRREL S.

I am asserting that Ovelia Otter is innocent of the crime as a result of her being a product of this forest and its legal and social and spiritual and educational systems.

PROSECUTOR LYNX

Ridiculous. That is absolutely NO defense. Do you suggest that we let Ovelia Otter back into the forest, back into the community she has so grievously transgressed? Punish, in effect, the rest of the community?

DEFENSE SQUIRREL S.

I do. They and you and she and I and you, Your Honor, are all to blame. We are all to blame. It's our fault. It's us.

PROSECUTOR LYNX
Pennstin was us.

DEFENSE SQUIRREL S.
Yes, she's us too. Absolutely.

PROSECUTOR LYNX
She WAS us.

DEFENSE SQUIRREL S.
Yes, of course.

JUDGE BODON BOAR
Enough! Are you presenting your closing arguments??

DEFENSE SQUIRREL S. & PROSECUTOR LYNX
NO!

JUDGE BODON BOAR
Allow Mr. Shellscape to step down and proceed to closing arguments.

DEFENSE SQUIRREL S.
Yes, Thank you, Mr. Shellscape please feel free to step down. But, Your Honor, I am going to call Ovelia Otter to the stand. May we take a break first, Your Honor?

JUDGE BODON BOAR
No! Let's finish this up. I'm losing my patience and the night is coming and I would like to get foraging.

DEFENSE SQUIRREL S.
Okay. Your Honor, I would like to call to the witness

stand the defendant Ovelia Otter.

JUDGE BODON BOAR
(rustling, clamoring, and worried looks from the jury) Jury, please settle yourself. Ms. Otter, will you align yourself with the intentions of veracity?

OVELIA OTTER
I will, Your Honor. Thank you.

DEFENSE SQUIRREL S.
Ovelia, thank you for testifying today.

OVELIA OTTER
Oh, no, thank you!

DEFENSE SQUIRREL S.
So, we've heard a lot about you and about what happened at Bear Chondra's Mix Flow Get Up And Go exercise class at the wishing well recently and we would like to hear your account of what happened.

OVELIA OTTER
Well, I don't know what else I can add. From what I've heard everybody saw it right and, you know, I'm just sorry. I'm sorry I put everyone through that and I'm sorry to young Pennstin and her family.

DEFENSE SQUIRREL S.
Well, we are all sorry for Pennstin but we are here to talk about your alleged participation in this unfortunate incident.

OVELIA OTTER

Well, I mean. I don't understand. I did it. I killed young Pennstin and everyone saw it and I just wish I hadn't. Every time I shut my eyes I see it all again. I just don't know why I would do myself and Pennstin such a lousy turn.

DEFENSE SQUIRREL S.

Okay, well, yes, that's what we'd like to get clear with. Just why did you do this?

OVELIA OTTER

I don't know.

PROSECUTOR LYNX

Your apologies and ignorance won't bring young Pennstin back to the forest. This show of contrition won't bring her sisters and brothers paw-to-paw with their kin! Never again, Ovelia, will young Pennstin the wolf feel the wet warmth of her mother's breath.

DEFENSE SQUIRREL S.

Objection! Your Honor, please ask that prosecution waits until their closing remarks to engage in this affective fallacy.

JUDGE BODON BOAR

Yes, please, Lynx, control yourself.

OVELIA OTTER

No, she is right to make me feel bad about this. Right to remind me of just how I've ruined everything. I've gotta say, though, I don't think you could be more effective in your shaming of me than I am.

DEFENSE SQUIRREL S.

Okay, okay, it is, of course, important that we see how sorrowful you are about this and I think this will go a long way in helping the woods recognize just how you are responding to this but again, I must say that we would like to get to the bottom of this unfortunate incident. Just why did this happen?

OVELIA OTTER

Okay, we were all there. We were all exercising together and listening and then *something* happened. Somehow the exercise and the focus on body and all that being actually alive! Turned me on. I mean on and on and on.

OVELIA speaks insistently without hysteria.

Have you ever, Your Honor, felt so actual, SO extant that it turns you on? I mean on and on and on??

JUDGE BODON BOAR

I have, Ovelia.

OVELIA OTTER

I mean, felt it so much, been so inside of the feeling of it that the edges of where you exist and who else exists and just what you are doing with the existing all fade away…like

Squeezing paws together hard.

the material of what is your life or another life or soil

or color or sound all are one, one, I don't know…not one thing, I don't want to say that, I mean, all so alive. So actual. So sexual with actual. Have you ever, Your Honor, hurt from actual? Hurt from alive?

JUDGE BODON BOAR
I have felt this pain. I have felt this pleasure. It can be too much to feel your body. Too much to know that it will end. Many is the night I pet hard my sweet companion.

JURORS
(sings/chants this behind JUDGE BODON BOAR's soliloquy) A dog, a cat, a dog, a dog, a cat, and then two cats and then one cat and a dog and then two cats and dog and a sickly dove. A parakeet so full of love.

JUDGE BODON BOAR
I pet it an eternity with pressure and gaze in its eyes and say or think or emanate, "You will be dead soon. You will no longer be with me here to bear this grave demoralization. No longer will the haptic lightning which your back and my large hoof construct light up the skies of our dreams! No longer will you walk. And no longer will you hear. No longer will I be so pleasantly brought elsewhere by your visage."

I have felt the pain of knowing my own body. Watching it change. Seeing it react. Moving it with empiricist surety. The pleasure of knowing my own body. My body has always been stupid. My body has always been holding itself. Waiting to be wanted before taking pleasure. Stupid body. Bad jokes. Awkward rustle through the forest brush hunting mushrooms in the night. Moved from space to space by the tunnel of scents and the map of intuition.

OVELIA OTTER

Yes, Your Honor, it's just this feeling. This edge between ecstasy and terror. This motion which is all about *life* that I was feeling. The too terrible presence of life and the burden and expectation of deep joy. I felt like a balloon filling and filling and filling with the awareness of life. When my teeth ripped into the warm flesh of young Pennstin I felt, at last, a release of that unbearable pressure. That thin and delicate membrane of want stretched to its very breaking point. Or, rather, I felt it break! I felt it release and subside and expire and calm. It was too painful, all that being alive. All that knowing what could be. Could be made or felt or done. Gravity alone is enough. The pulling of possibility was simply too painful. I do not know why I turned towards Pennstin. Perhaps because her age and simple wonder and hope seemed the embodiment of all that will bring pain. Her lovely inquisitiveness and delicate phalanges. Her positive and open nature and steadfast attention to detail. She was exquisitely present in a way which forebodes great pain. And she was wonderfully soft with a glowing yellow coat. I felt no ill will towards her or her family which I have met several times on the road through the dell. They are a touching clan with an intimate ferocity I admire. Her eyes so always looking. Perhaps it was that looking what set me off in class. I remember there was an awful lot of blood and as it poured out of her and poured out of my mouth and off of my claws and soaked into my fur and the ground beneath us I felt the absolution that her warm liquid extinction provided. Not absolution for the crime. I don't even care...put me in a box or make me clean the stones or sever my paws from my body so that I may never hurt again nor never hold the paw of my sweet sister as Pennstin will never hold the paws of her kin...I do not want forgiveness.

Courtroom freezes for a long time. Slowly, a song...

JURORS
(singing as deliberation until the judge stands)
The absolution that Pennstin's blood provided
Was something entirely different

BISON
It was something that she needed

TURTLE
Something she had to have

LIZARD
To her guilt she has conceded

HARRISON HARE
To Pennstin's kin that ain't no salve

FERN CARDINAL
The spaces between life and death are fraught

LIZARD
To resist the need to answer she had fought

TIGER SEPET & HARRISON HARE
But she lost the fight and answer, whoa, she did
And because she answered we lost that cute wolf kid

FERN CARDINAL & LIZARD
Guilting Ovelia won't bring back Pennstin
She's on the other side now with her passed kin
Maybe we let this one slide and rebegin
I don't think we need to believe in sin

TIGER SEPET & HARRISON HARE
That's preposterous, we'll wreak havoc on the woods
We gotta reinforce that we follow rules that's good
Make an example of this otter I think we should
We don't kill other animals if not for food

TURTLE
I don't know how they think we can figure this out

BISON
Did I tell you I saw a two-headed trout?

TURTLE & BISON
(rolling around)
Ha ha ha ha
Ha ha ha ha
Ha ha ha ha
Ha ha ha ha

FERN CARDINAL & LIZARD
(behind the laughter)
Have you no mercy?
She is clearly contrite

TIGER SEPET & HARRISON HARE

Can you not see
That what she did was not right?

FERN CARDINAL & LIZARD

Is not the sense of right and wrong
A little childish?

TIGER SEPET & HARRISON HARE

A world without these
Would be pretty hellish

FERN CARDINAL & LIZARD

The hubris of calling someone guilty's not in us

TIGER SEPET & HARRISON HARE

Well why didn't you address that in *voir dire?*
We've all wasted a lot of time here

FERN CARDINAL & LIZARD

We didn't know all the places it would go
We didn't know by the end we would not know

TIGER SEPET & HARRISON HARE

But there's really not much to consider
You were there in the class you watched her

BISON

(to TURTLE) Remember it was loud and gory

TURTLE

I think Bear Chondra was telling a story

BISON

I remember you shook your tail at me

TURTLE

I remember feeling pretty happy

BISON

Is there a word for when you're in the water?

TURTLE

You mean the way your eyes begin to feel softer?

BISON

I always like to feel my hooves in grass

TURTLE

I like to implicate my ass

BISON

Let's take a nap while they work this out

TURTLE

They got some more opinions they need to flout

TURTLE & BISON

Ha ha ha ha ha…

Ha, ha, ha continues as instrumental background.

FERN CARDINAL & LIZARD

(counterpoint to BISON & TURTLE)
It's not nothing to
Decide what we should do

The questions of right and wrong
Are too complex to sing in song
And too nuanced to balance on
Even though we do not condone
We don't feel comfortable condemning
We won't condemn

TIGER SEPET & HARRISON HARE

Don't deny your role in
The greater whole
Your community needs you to
Do what you said you'd do
It's your chance to take a stand
Help to build a peaceful land
We will not acquit
Our conscience won't let us do it
We won't acquit

*Jury ends song. JUDGE BODON BOAR stands up.
Everyone looks to the judge, waiting.*

JUDGE BODON BOAR

I have no choice but to declare this a mistrial.

*Gasps from the gallery, TIGER SEPET & HARRISON
HARE irate.*

PROSECUTOR LYNX

This is an outrage! This is repugnant!! There is no
question in the forest that Ms. Otter brutally and for
NO REASON killed young Pennstin the wolf. Your
Honor, I will have you sanctioned! We will appeal!

JUDGE BODON BOAR

That is your right, and I understand your anger, but I too am bound by the law and if this jury, after much and careful deliberation, is unable to reach an agreement, I am bound to declare a mistrial. In the words of the human songbird D'Angelo, "Ain't no justice, just us."

BLACK OUT / END OF SCENE.

ACT 2 | SCENE 13

SETTING: *A clearing in the woods outside the courthouse.*

AT RISE: *REPORTER ELLE E. PHANT is in front of the news camera with the microphone to her mouth.*

REPORTER ELLE E. PHANT

Okay, wow! An unexpected and unpopular verdict handed down by the judge. What we have here is an example of the woods' inability to come to any—

Interrupted by DEAD/GHOST PENNSTIN who walks in front of ELLE E. PHANT. She is dead and bloody and sings from D'Angelo's "Devil's Pie":

DEAD/GHOST PENNSTIN

"I know I was born to die
Searching to find a peace of mind"

BLACK OUT / END OF PLAY.

ABOUT THE AUTHOR

Stephanie Barber is a writer and artist who has created a poetic, conceptual and philosophical body of work in a variety of media, often literary/visual hybrids that dissolve boundaries between narrative, essay, and dialectic works. Her work considers the basic questions of human existence (its morbidity, profundity, and banality) with play and humor.

ACKNOWLEDGMENTS

I would like to thank Sarah Jacklin for originally commissioning this play, my sisters Cate Barber and Llana Barber for reading and discussing early versions of the project, and Adam Robinson for pointing me in the direction of Plays Inverse.

This book is in solemn memory of my beautiful neighbors Joyce Anderson and Alex Bland.